LITERATURE AND CRITICAL THINKING

Art Projects • Bulletin Boards • Plot Summaries
Skill Building Activities • Independent Thinking

Written by: Patty Carratello
Illustrated by: Theresa Wright, Linda Smythe, and Blanqui Apodaca

HOW TO EAT FRIED WORMS

THE WHIPPING BOY

THE TROUBLE WITH TUCK

HELP! I'M A PRISONER IN THE LIBRARY

CALL IT COURAGE

BE A PERFECT PERSON IN JUST THREE DAYS

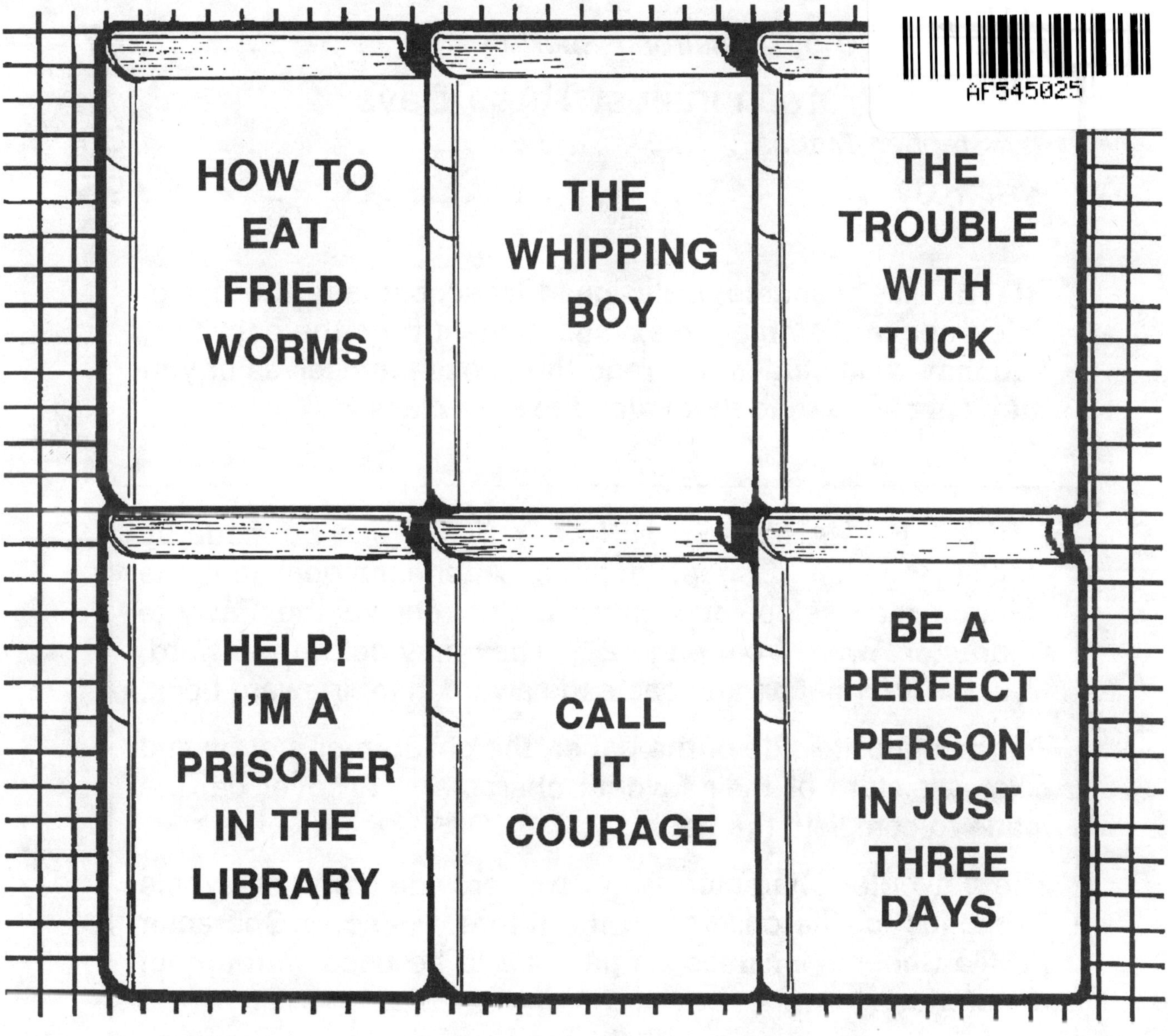

Teacher Created Materials, Inc.
P. O. Box 1214
Huntington Beach, CA 92649

Made in U.S.A.

ISBN 1-55734-359-4

TABLE OF CONTENTS

NOTE: This resource is designed to accompany the books listed above. To obtain maximum benefit from the activities, you may want students to read the books themselves or you may choose to read them aloud to your class.

FAVORITE CHARACTER MEMORY BOOK can be made by stapling together 12 sheets of paper. After each book unit, the children may select one character to receive the Favorite Character Award from page 21. They may color the award, fill in the information and paste the award in their award book.

On the opposite side of the paper, the children can draw and color a picture of their favorite character. A cover can be made to complete the book.

The Favorite Character Book will provide very enjoyable memories for the children in the future. Also, a Character Profile Sheet is included on page 22 to be used with any of the stories.

INTRODUCTION

LITERATURE AND CRITICAL THINKING

It is possible for all children at varying developmental levels to engage in a discovery process which clarifies thinking, increases knowledge, and deepens their understanding of human issues and social values. This activities book, based on Bloom's *Taxonomy of Skills in the Cognitive Domain*, provides teachers a resource to maximize this process, using distinguished children's literature as a vehicle.

The authors suggest the following options in using this book:

OPTION 1: The teacher may select a single activity for the entire class.

OPTION 2: The teacher may select different activities for single students or small groups of students.

OPTION 3: The student may select the level at which he or she wishes to work, once the teacher explains what is available.

The stories in this book follow the same format, so that each level of thinking skills is approached as follows:

KNOWLEDGE

This level provides the child with an opportunity to recall fundamental facts and information about the story. Success at this level will be evidenced by the child's ability to:

- Match character names with pictures of the characters.
- Identify the main characters in a crossword puzzle.
- Match statements with the characters who said them.
- List the main characteristics of one of the main characters in a WANTED poster.
- Arrange scrambled story pictures in sequential order.
- Arrange scrambled story sentences in sequential order.
- Recall details about the setting by creating a picture of where a part of the story took place.

COMPREHENSION

This level provides the child with an opportunity to demonstrate a basic understanding of the story. Success at this level will be evidenced by the child's ability to:

- Interpret pictures of scenes from the story.
- Explain selected ideas or parts from the story in his or her own words.

COMPREHENSION (Continued)

- Draw a picture showing what happened before and after a passage or illustration found in the book.
- Write a sentence explaining what happened before and after a passage or illustration found in the book.
- Predict what *could* happen next in the story before the reading of the entire book is completed.
- Construct a pictorial time line which summarizes what happens in the story.
- Explain how the main character felt at the beginning, middle, and/or end of the story.

APPLICATION

This level provides the child with an opportunity to use information from the story in a new way. Success at this level will be evidenced by the child's ability to:

- Classify the characters as human, animal, or thing.
- Transfer a main character to a new setting.
- Make finger puppets and act out a part of the story.
- Select a meal that one of the main characters would enjoy eating, plan a menu, and a method of serving it.
- Think of a situation that occurred to a character in the story and write about how he or she would have handled the situation differently.
- Give examples of people the child knows who have the same problems as the characters in the story.

ANALYSIS

This level provides the child with an opportunity to take parts of the story and examine these parts carefully in order to better understand the whole story. Success at this level will be evidenced by the child's ability to:

- Identify general characteristics (stated and/or implied) of the main characters.
- Distinguish what could happen from what couldn't happen in the story in real life.
- Select parts of the story that were funniest, saddest, happiest, and most unbelievable.
- Differentiate fact from opinion.
- Compare and/or contrast two of the main characters.
- Select an action of a main character that was exactly the same as something the child would have done.

SYNTHESIS

This level provides the child with an opportunity to put parts from the story together in a new way to form a new idea or product. Success at this level will be evidenced by the child's ability to:

- Create a story from just the title before the story is read (pre-story exercise).
- Write three new titles for the story that would give a good idea what it was about.
- Create a poster to advertise the story so people will want to read it.
- Create a new product related to the story.
- Restructure the roles of the main characters to create new outcomes in the story.
- Compose and perform a dialogue or monologue that will communicate the thoughts of the main character(s) at a given point in the story.
- Imagine that he or she is one of the main characters and write a diary account of daily thoughts and activities.
- Create an original character and tell how the character would fit into the story.
- Write the lyrics and music to a song that one of the main characters would sing if he/she/it became a rock star — and perform it.

EVALUATION

This level provides the child with an opportunity to form and present an opinion backed up by sound reasoning. Success at the level will be evidenced by the child's ability to:

- Decide which character in the selection he or she would most like to spend a day with and why.
- Judge whether or not a character should have acted in a particular way and why.
- Decide if the story really could have happened and justify reasons for the decision.
- Consider how this story can help the child in his or her own life.
- Appraise the value of the story.
- Compare this story with another one the child has read.
- Write a recommendation as to why the books should be read or not.

In addition to the activities just outlined, a class project and a small groups project will be included for each story.

How to Eat Fried Worms

by Thomas Rockwell

Alan bets Billy fifty dollars that he can't eat fifteen worms. Well, fifty dollars is a lot of money for a boy Billy's age. Fifty dollars can buy Billy that used minibike he wants. So Billy takes the bet!

Armed with condiments like mustard, ketchup, and horseradish, he eats the first worm — and it isn't as bad as he thought it would be. Realizing that Billy might actually be able to eat the fifteen worms, Alan begins to panic. He tries every devious trick imaginable to discourage Billy from going through with the bet. At one point he becomes so desperate that he even glues two worms together, hoping that Billy will be unable to consume such a formidable feast.

Billy manages to thwart Alan's tricks and goes on to win the bet. In the process, however, he becomes so accustomed to the taste of worms that, even after the bet is over, we find him enjoying a worm-and-egg on rye sandwich.

KNOWLEDGE: Activity 1

DESCRIPTIONS

Write the characters' names under their descriptions.

Tom	Alan	Billy	Joe

CHUNKY
SNUB-NOSED
FRECKLED
DARE-TAKER

SMALL
KNOBBY-KNEED
RED HAIR
MESSY
UNTIED SHOES
NERVOUS
MONEY IN THE BANK

1. ____________________

2. ____________________

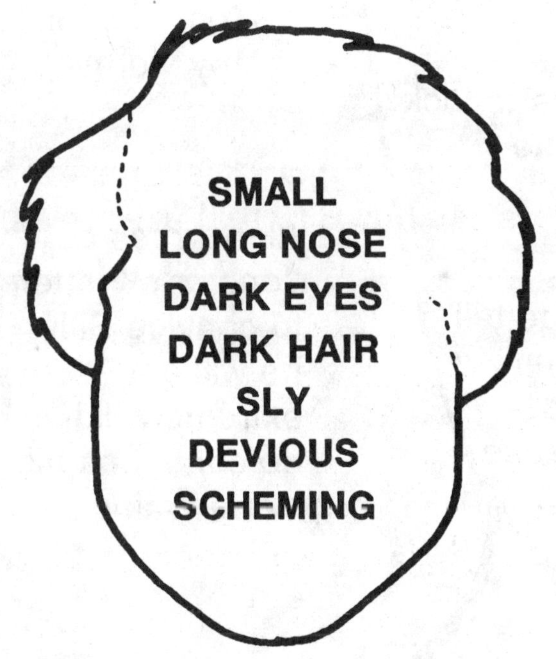

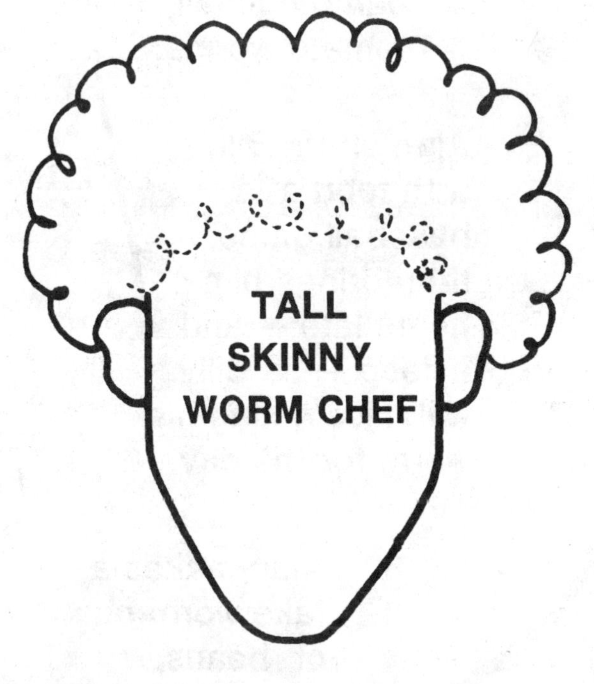

3. ____________________

4. ____________________

KNOWLEDGE: Activity 2

THIS BET IS OVER!

Alan begins to realize early on that Billy actually **can** eat 15 worms. So he tries to find ways to end the bet before Billy can win.

Circle the ways Alan uses.

1. Alan tells Billy he can eat small, tomato worms.
2. Alan stuffs Billy with food at a baseball game, then brings him home late — and asleep — so Billy will miss eating his worm for the day.
3. Alan makes a fake worm out of beans.
4. Alan and Joe tell Billy's mother what Billy is eating because of their bet.
5. Alan tries to lock Billy in the cistern.
6. Alan says Billy can not use ketchup, mustard, or anything on the worms.
7. Alan glues two worms together.
8. Alan and Joe use worms from the manure pile.
9. Alan will not allow Billy and Tom to cook any worms.
10. Alan writes a "doctor's" letter to convice Billy he will get extremely ill if he continues his worm eating.

COMPREHENSION: Activity 1

WHAT HAPPENS?

Look at this picture. Explain what occurs in the story to make this picture happen. Also describe what happens right after this picture.

BEFORE:________________________________

AFTER:________________________________

COMPREHENSION: Activity 2

WHAT HAPPENED?

What happens in the story to make the characters say or do these things?

1. *"A night crawler isn't a **worm**! If it was a worm, it'd be called a worm. A night crawler's a night crawler."* (Billy to Joe, Alan, and Tom) ____________________

2. *"Hello. We're Alan Phelps and Joseph O'Hara. We're the reason you were waked up in the middle of the night last night, and we're sorry."* (Alan and Joe to neighbors) ____________________

3. *"Do you think there's something the doctors don't know? Do you think I could be the first person who's ever been **hooked** on worms?"* (Billy to Tom and Joe) ____________________

APPLICATION: Activity 1 **CLASS PROJECT**

WORM COOKBOOK

Plan a worm recipe that could make a worm taste delicious. Put your recipe in a **Worm Cookbook**, along with the other recipes created by students in your class. Then try your recipes, using **spaghetti** for worms!

My Favorite Worm Recipe

by ____________________

YUK!

- Make a list of ten things you hate to eat. Then, put a star (☆) next to the three things you dislike the most.

1. ______________________
2. ______________________
3. ______________________
4. ______________________
5. ______________________
6. ______________________
7. ______________________
8. ______________________
9. ______________________
10. ______________________

- Trade papers with your neighbors. Circle three items on your neighbor's list that you like least. It's O.K. to circle the starred items.
- Trade papers back. You now have your own paper.
- Report the starred and circled items to your teacher. He or she will write the "yuk" foods on the chalkboard, eliminating any duplications from other classmates.
- Choose the three "yukiest" things from the class list. Write them on the ballot below.
- Cut the ballot from this paper and give it to your teacher. Your teacher will record the ballot votes on the board to determine the class "yukiest" winners!

YUK BALLOT

These are the three yukiest things to eat:

1. ______________________
2. ______________________
3. ______________________

ANALYSIS: Activity 1

TALK, TALK, TALK!

Tom tells Billy to "think fish, fish, fish" as a way to get him to eat a worm.

What three things could you say to a friend to get him or her to eat a worm?

1. ______________________________

2. ______________________________

3. ______________________________

What three things could you say to a friend to discourage him or her from eating a worm?

1. ______________________________

2. ______________________________

3. ______________________________

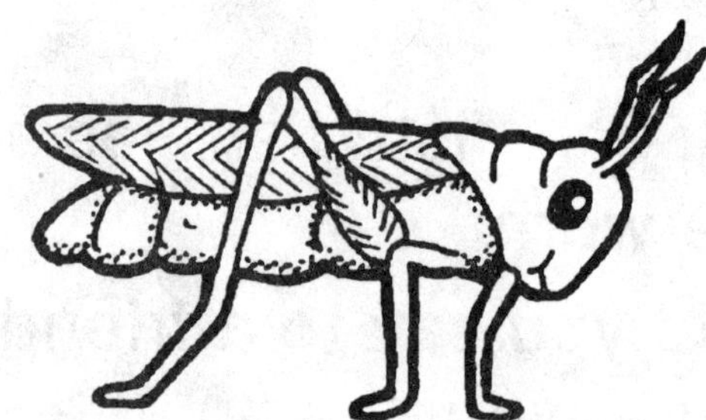

ONE BITE!

Billy says, "One bite can't hurt you. I'd eat one bite of anything before I'd let them send me up to my room right after supper."

Would you? Read this list of things. Separate them into two lists — the things you would be willing to eat and the things you would never eat. Write these lists on page 2.

moldy bread	raw fish	beetles
dog biscuits	chicken eggs	pepper
chocolate	bananas	sand
burnt toast	tofu	cereal
fingernails	octopus	grapes
grasshoppers	yogurt	broccoli
beef tongue	spinach	hot sauce
ice cream	beans	baby food
dirt	olives	peas
snails	ants	pizza
pig's feet	liver	vitamins
rotten eggs	frog's legs	raisins
paper	buttermilk	mustard
worms	popcorn	rice

ONE BITE!

I would eat:

I would *never* eat:

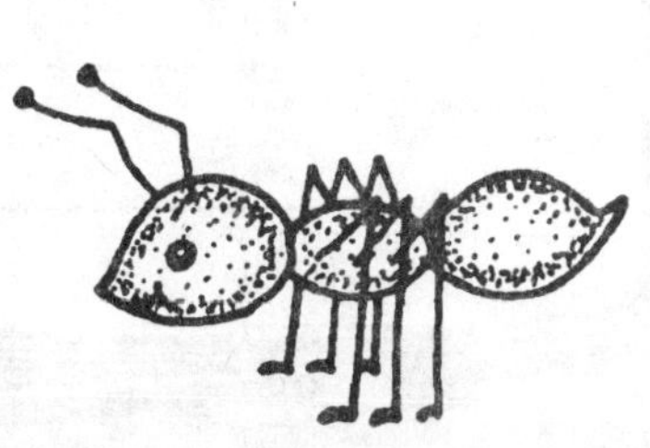

HOW TO EAT FRIED WORMS

You will be reading a book called ***How To Eat Fried Worms***. Write your ideas for what a story with this title might be like. Draw an illustration for the book cover, too.

How to Eat Fried Worms

by ____________________

____

Summary of story

____

____

____

____

____

____

____

____

____

____

____

____

____

MAKE IT CLEAR!

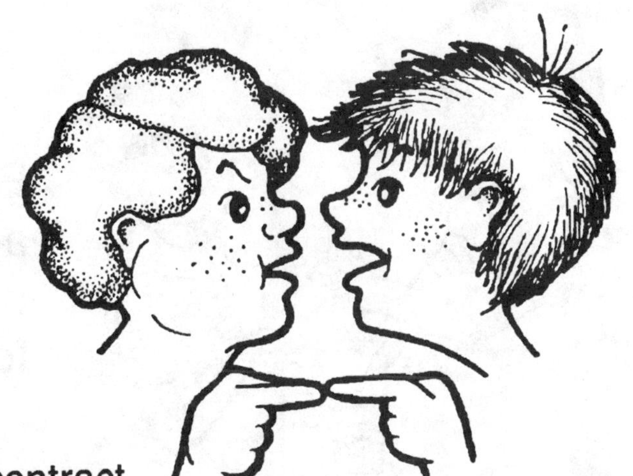

When Billy and Alan made their bet, they made an agreement to do something. It is a wise thing, when two people make an agreement, for both people to be clear about the rules, or the terms of their agreement. The terms of their agreement are then written in a contract.

Billy and Alan obviously didn't have a contract because they kept arguing over the terms of their agreement. That was because the terms of their agreement were **unclear**. If they had made the terms of their agreement **clear** to begin with, they could have avoided their arguing.

Directions:

1. With another person, write a contract that Billy and Alan could have used for their bet. One of you be Billy, and the other be Alan. Go back and reread the story to find the problems in their agreement — that is, where the terms were unclear. When you find an unclear term, write it so that it is clear (make sure you both agree to it). Do this on a separate piece of paper or on the back of this paper.

   FOR EXAMPLE:

   Unclear: Alan will get the worms for Billy to eat.

   Clear: Alan will get the worms for Billy to eat. However, he may only get them from the garden in front of Billy's house. And, he may only get them when Billy or Tom is with him.

2. On the contract form your teacher gives you, recopy the terms of "your" agreement. The first one is done for you. If you run out of space for your terms, you may continue on the back of the contract form.
3. Both of you sign and date the agreement. Get a witness to sign also.

CONTRACT

Billy Forrester and Alan Phelps agree that Alan will pay Billy fifty dollars if Billy eats one worm a day for fifteen days in a row.

TERMS OF THE AGREEMENT

1. *Alan will get the worms for Billy to eat. However, he may only get them from the garden in front of Billy's house. And, he may only get them when Billy or Tom is with him.*
2. ______________________________
3. ______________________________
4. ______________________________
5. ______________________________

Billy and Alan agree to the terms listed above.

______________________ ______________

Billy Forrester Date

______________________ ______________ ______________________

Alan Phelps Date **Witness**

EVALUATION: Activity 1

PARENTS

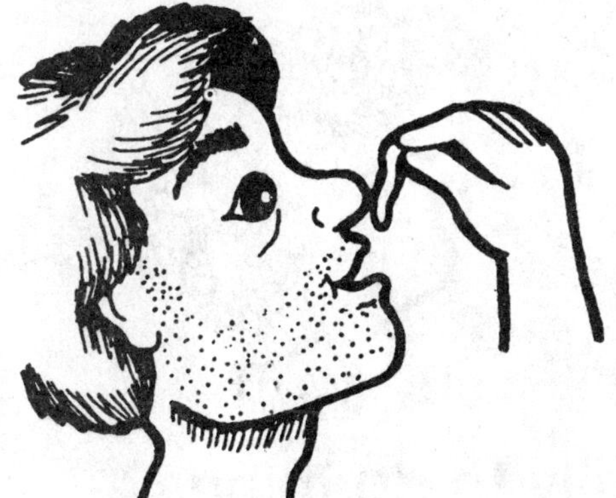

Billy's parents support him in what he is doing, even though they do not agree that eating worms is right. Billy's mother even creates recipes for Billy to make his worms tastier.

1. Do you think Billy's parents are like most parents? ________
   What would your mother say to you if you told her you were eating worms? ______________________________
   ____
   ____

2. Would she let you continue? ______________
   Why? ______________________________
   ____
   ____
   ____
   ____

3. What would your father say to you if you told him you were eating worms? ______
   ____
   ____

4. Would he let you continue? ______________
   Why? ______________________________
   ____
   ____
   ____
   ____

5. Would you let your own children eat worms? ________
   Why? ______________________________
   ____
   ____
   ____
   ____
   ____
   ____

I DARE YOU!

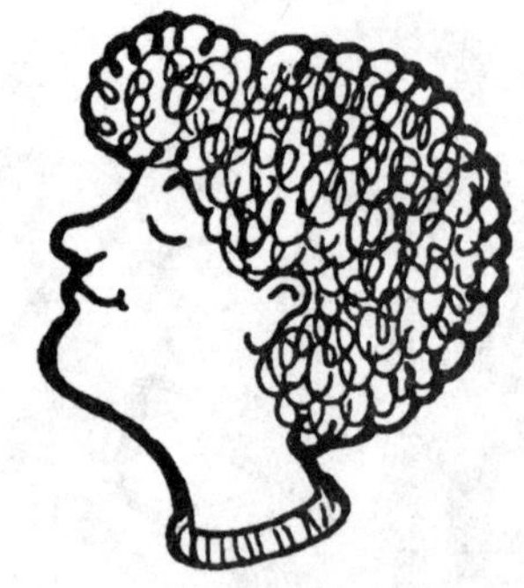

People are always daring Billy to do things and Billy accepts their dares.

1. Why do you think people like to dare Billy to do things? ______________________________

2. Why do you think Billy accepts their dares? ______________________________

3. One reason people accept dares is to prove they are okay. Do you feel that you are okay? ____________

   Explain. ____________

4. Do you ever wish that you were bigger, smarter, quieter, more attractive, braver, funnier, more athletic, smaller, more talkative, or more popular than you are? ____________

   Explain. ______________________________

5. Would you accept a dare to prove you are okay? ____________

   Explain. ______________________________

EVALUATION: Favorite Character Memory Book

I LIKE...

Which one of the characters in the story do you like best? ____________

Why? ____________

____

Which of the characters in the story do you like least? ____________

____

Why? ____________

____

Make an award for your favorite character.
Fill in the blanks on the ribbon.
Color the ribbon and cut it out.
Put the ribbon in your Favorite Character memory book.

(See page 2)

character's name →

your name →

a few words about your character →

book and author →

Favorite Character Award
presented to
____
by
____
because you are
____
____

Author: ____________ ____________

Book: ____________ ____________

CHARACTER PROFILE

Develop one of the main characters in the story into a real person. As you fill in these blanks, try to be in the mind of the character.

Book ______________________________

Author ______________________________

Name of Character ______________________________

Age______Height_____Weight_____Male or Female ______

Hair Color ______Eye Color ______ Skin Color __________

1. Where does he/she live? ______________________________
2. What kind of job does he/she have or would like to have?

   ____

   Why?______________________________

   ____
3. Who is his/her best friend?______________________________
4. Does he/she have any enemies?______________________________

   ____
5. Does he/she like life?______________________________

   ____
6. Fill in these blanks with his/her favorites.

   Color ____________________ Food ____________________

   Animal ____________________ Hobby____________________

   Sport ____________________ Music ____________________

   Place to go ______________________________

   Thing to do ______________________________
7. Would you like to have this character as a friend?________

   Explain______________________________

   ____

The Whipping Boy

by Sid Fleishman

Mischief-making Prince Horace, known to his subjects as Prince Brat, flaunts his insolent and prankish behavior. His actions infuriate his father, the King, and cause whipping boy Jemmy to take punishment in the Prince's place. An especially painful time for Jemmy is during the Prince's daily lessons, for Prince Brat refuses to learn his letters and numbers and Jemmy receives the tutor's ire, lash by lash. But between the lashings, Jemmy becomes literate.

One evening, bored with his life, Prince Brat decides to run away, taking Jemmy with him. They are stopped by cutthroat thieves, who upon seeing the King's crest on the horse and hearing Prince Brat's proud, but ill-timed declaration of royalty, decide to hold them for ransom. However, the writing of the ransom note reveals Jemmy's literacy, and so confuses the thieves that they assume Jemmy to be the Prince and Prince Brat to be the whipping boy.

This mistaken identity gives Jemmy and Prince Brat an opportunity to learn much about each other and the meaning of friendship. They have a dangerous, but grand adventure together, meeting and making friends, confounding thieves, and learning to respect each other.

KNOWLEDGE: Activity 1

CHARACTER CROSSWORD

Complete this crossword puzzle. Use the wordbox to help you.

Brat	Master Peckwit	Cutwater	Smudge
King	Johnny Tosher	Petunia	Billy
Nips	Prince Horace	Jemmy	Betsy

DOWN

1. Billy's partner
2. The Whipping Boy
4. Real name of the boy who did not learn to read and write, even though he had lessons
5. Man who was very tired of his son's mischief
6. Kind of hot-potato man, Captain ____________
9. Name the Prince was called behind his back

ACROSS

3. Royal tutor who tried to teach the Prince
7. Mean thief who smelled like garlic
8. Girl who owned a dancing bear
10. Man who directed the thieves the wrong way in the sewer
11. Bear who scared the thieves away from Jemmy and the Prince
12. Jemmy's rat-catching friend who shook the Prince's hand

KNOWLEDGE: Activity 2

PATH OF EVENTS

Here are six things that happen in the story. Cut them out and paste them in story order along the path on the next page. Under the events, write the names of the characters in them.

KNOWLEDGE: Activity 2 (Continued)

PATH OF EVENTS

Paste the events in story order. With the events, write the names of the characters in them.

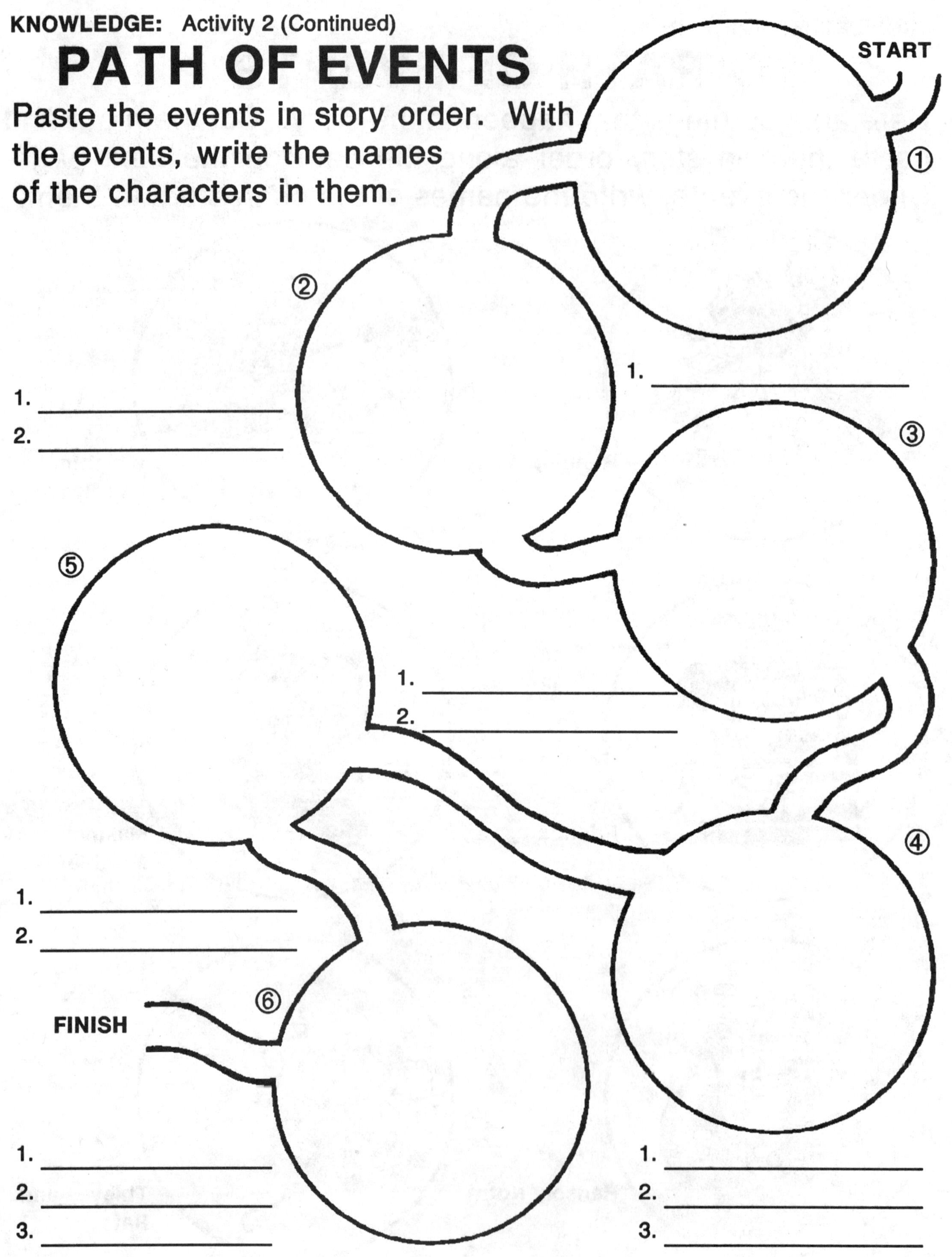

COMPREHENSION: Activity 1

WORDS, WORDS, WORDS!

Read these sentences from the story. Circle the definition of each underlined word.

1. "But all the while he was feeling a growing *exasperation* with his whipping boy."
   a) deep respect b) great irritation
   c) friendship

2. "Cutwater *rummaged* around in a black oak chest of stolen goods."
   a) searched actively b) played happily
   c) sat greedily

3. "Jemmy lifted his chin *arrogantly* and tried to look as prince-like as possible."
   a) with overbearing pride b) with pain c) quickly

4. "I'm thinking these lads have mixed themselves up to *flummox* us."
   a) anger b) amuse c) confuse

5. "Jemmy shot a *calculating* glance at Prince Brat."
   a) evaluating b) incriminating c) sympathetic

6. "As soon as the wheels rattled on cobbled street, Jemmy felt an *immense* sense of relief."
   a) frightened b) tearful c) enormous

7. "And then the news seller appeared, his tongue wagging like a bell clapper, a bundle of *broadsides* under his arm."
   a) telephone books b) printed papers c) magazines

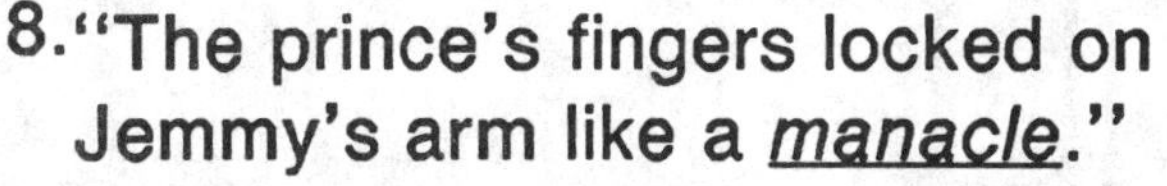

8. "The prince's fingers locked on Jemmy's arm like a *manacle*."
   a) poisonous spider
   b) type of octopus
   c) handcuff

COMPREHENSION: Activity 2

IN OTHER WORDS

Explain what each of these quotes mean in the context of the story.

1. "You betrayed me! . . . Ain't it me they think is the Prince? If you hadn't pointed me out under the straw, Cutwater would have flown off to pick up my tracks. And we could have crept away dead easy." — Jemmy

2. "Baw! Out!" Jemmy shouted. He'd dreamed of seeing the prince whipped, but now that it was happening, he found no satisfaction in it." — Jemmy

3. "If you boys decide to run away again, take me with you." — King

APPLICATION: Activity 1

IN OUR TIME

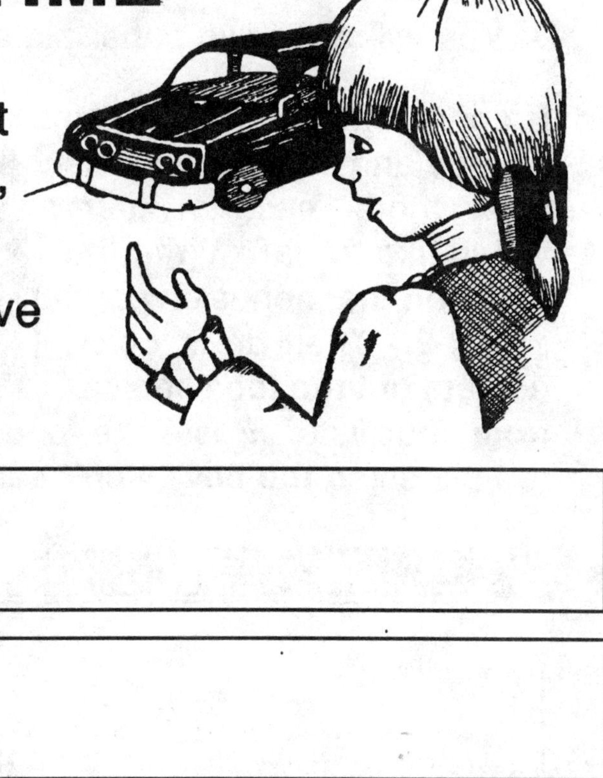

Prince Brat has moved from the past to our time. He still can **not** read, write, or do sums.

List at least 5 problems he would have today without these skills.

①

②

③

④

⑤

✲ Could he have someone else do any of these things for him? Choose one from your list. Explain how someone **could** or **could not** do this for him.

____

____

____

____

____

APPLICATION: Activity 2 (Page 1 of 2)

MENUS FOR TWO

✘ You will need two paper plates, construction paper, glue, and scissors

1. Prepare meals for Prince Horace and Jemmy. Decide what foods each of them would like to eat. Write the foods on the menus on page 1 and 2. Then draw, color, and cut out the food choices from your lists. Paste the foods on the boys' paper plates. Be sure to label the plates so the boys won't eat the wrong meals!

Menu
for
Prince Horace

______________________	______________________
______________________	______________________
______________________	______________________
______________________	______________________
______________________	______________________
______________________	______________________
______________________	______________________
______________________	______________________
______________________	______________________
______________________	______________________
______________________	______________________

APPLICATION: Activity 2 (Page 2 of 2)

MENUS FOR TWO

Menu
for
Jemmy

______________________ ______________________

______________________ ______________________

______________________ ______________________

______________________ ______________________

______________________ ______________________

______________________ ______________________

______________________ ______________________

______________________ ______________________

______________________ ______________________

______________________ ______________________

______________________ ______________________

2. Cut out and paste these name tags on the correct plates.

Jemmy

JEMMY AND HORACE

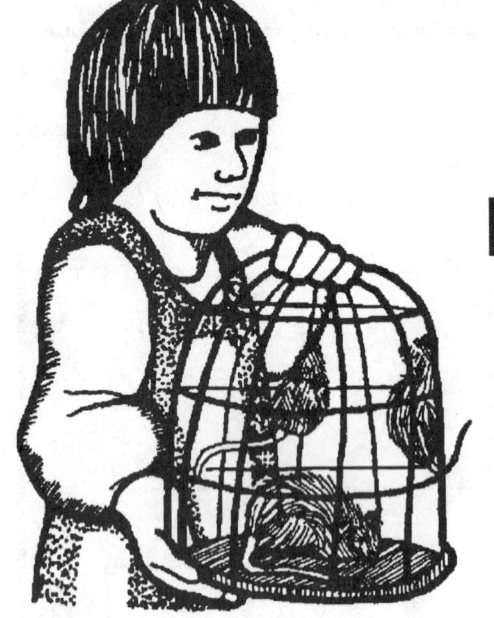

Alike and Different!

1. In what ways are Jemmy and Horace alike?

____

____

____

____

2. In what ways are Jemmy and Horace different?

____

____

____

____

3. Do you think they are **more** alike or **more** different?

____

Why? ____

____

____

____

____

WHAT IS A FRIEND?

1. What makes two people friends? Write any ideas you have here. Work with a partner. ____________________

2. What makes Prince Horace and Jemmy friends? Write your ideas here. ____________________

3. You and your partner will pretend to be Prince Horace and Jemmy. Write reasons why you like each other here.

   I like Jemmy because ____________________

   I like Prince Horace because ____________________

4. Give your reasons for this friendship in front of the class! (One of you will be the Prince, and one of you will be Jemmy.)

SYNTHESIS: Activity 1

A DAY IN THE LIFE OF PRINCE HORACE

Imagine you are Prince Horace. What would a daily activity schedule be like for you before the story? What would a day be like for you after the story?

My Schedule (before)  by Prince Horace	My Schedule (after)  by Prince Horace

RANSOM NOTE!

Suppose it was up to you to write the ransom note to the King.

1. What would you tell him? How much ransom would the King pay the thieves for the life of Prince Horace?
2. Write your note here.

RANSOM NOTE

3. How would this note be delivered to the King? ____________
____
____
____

4. Now, read your ransom note BACKWARDS to the class. As you read, each class member will write your words. See how many classmates can decipher your note!

CHANGES

When characters in a story learn from their experiences, they grow as people. Sometimes this growth makes them change the way they are and what they do.

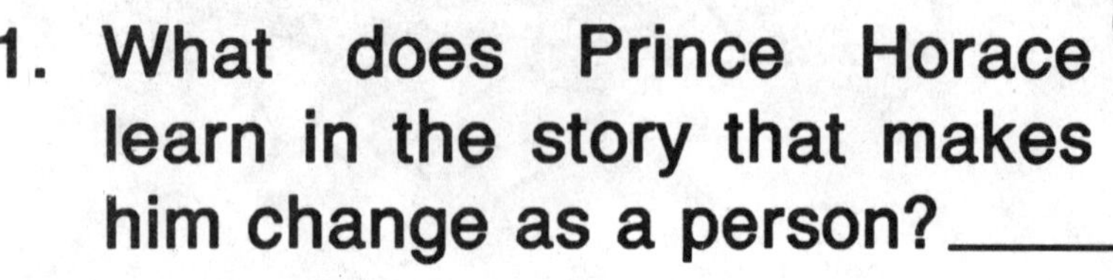

1. What does Prince Horace learn in the story that makes him change as a person? ________________

____

____

____

____

____

2. What does Jemmy learn in the story that makes him change as a person? __________

____

____

____

____

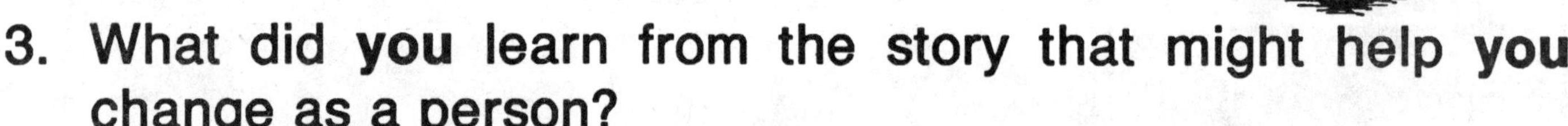

3. What did **you** learn from the story that might help **you** change as a person? ______________________

____

____

____

____

____

____

____

____

EVALUATION: Activity 2

CUSTOM

★ It was the custom, as the story goes, to keep a whipping boy to take the punishments that were really meant for a misbehaving prince.

1. Do you feel this custom was right? Explain your answer ______________________________

2. Why do you think this custom was started in the first place? ______________________________

3. Why do you think this custom is no longer in practice? ______________________________

★ A custom is the habit of doing something a certain way. Countries have customs, as do cities, schools, families, and special groups.

1. Can you think of a custom that is in practice today that should not be? ______________________________

2. What is this custom? ______________________________

3. Why should it not be in practice? ______________________________

4. Can you do anything to change this custom? ______________________________

The Trouble with Tuck

by Theodore Taylor

When her faithful dog Tuck runs through the kitchen screen door, thirteen-year-old Helen begins to worry. Tuck has never done anything like this before. She and her mom suspect that something is wrong with Tuck's eyes. And, a trip to the veterinarian confirms the suspicion.

Tuck, however, continues to go on his daily walks around the neighborhood as he always has — by himself. Helen, knowing her dog is living dangerously, suggests to her parents that Tuck get a seeing eye dog. But, when she only gets skeptical looks for her suggestion, she takes it upon herself to contact an institute that trains seeing eye dogs. She arranges a meeting with the institute and her parents — a meeting that brings disappointment.

It isn't until after a near-fatal accident in which Tuck gets hit by a car, that Mrs. Chaffey, the woman who works at the institute, calls them. She remembers Tuck and the disappointed little girl, and has a dog for Tuck. The dog's name is Lady Daisy, a brown and black German shepherd.

Tuck objects for a long time to the "intruder" until Helen devises a way to train him to follow Daisy. It works, and Tuck grins with delight, with a proud Helen cheering his new-found "sight."

KNOWLEDGE: Activity 1

TUCK IS BLIND

Helen knows that Tuck is blind. Several events lead her to this conclusion. Put these events in chronological order.

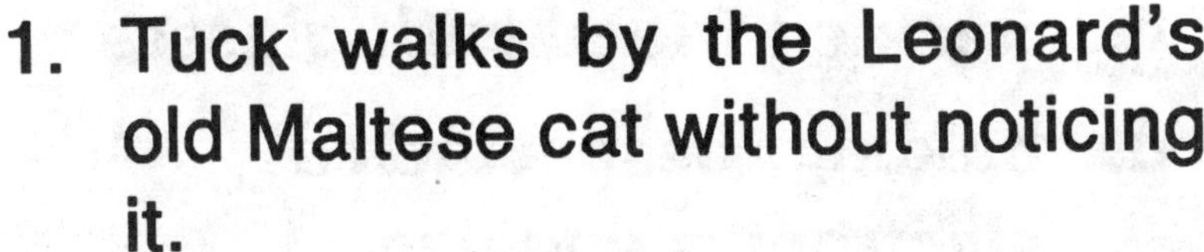

1. Tuck walks by the Leonard's old Maltese cat without noticing it.

2. Helen's mom tests Tuck's vision by putting a chair in front of the door.
3. Dr. Tobin examines Tuck.
4. Tuck stops chasing the doves in the back yard.
5. Tuck crashes through the screen door to chase after cats.

☆ ☆ ☆ ☆ ☆ ☆ ☆ ☆ ☆ ☆ ☆ ☆ ☆ ☆

1. ______________________________

2. ______________________________

3. ______________________________

4. ______________________________

5. ______________________________

MATCH THEM!

Match these characters with their descriptions.

1. _____ Helen Ogden
2. _____ Barbara Ogden
3. _____ Tony Ogden
4. _____ Stan Ogden
5. _____ Luke Ogden
6. _____ Dr. Tobin
7. _____ Steffie Pylee
8. _____ Mrs. Chaffey
9. _____ Mr. Ishibara
10. _____ Harry Peterson
11. _____ Tuck
12. _____ Daisy

a. attractive older brother
b. German shepherd guide dog
c. freckled friend with glasses
d. balding, bespectacled electronics engineer
e. optimistic vegetable produce manager
f. shy, freckled whistler
g. caring veterinarian
h. ball-playing younger brother
i. blind golden Labrador
j. pretty, auburn-haired teacher
k. administrator of companion dog school
l. dog trainer

COMPREHENSION: Activity 1

THE GIFT

Why does Tony Ogden give his daughter, Helen, the gift in this picture?

COMPREHENSION: Activity 2

THE PROMISE

Helen says to Tuck, "You've always taken care of me, and I'll always take care of you."

Describe two ways that Tuck takes care of Helen.

1. ____

____

2. ____

____

____

Describe two ways that Helen takes care of Tuck.

1. ____

____

2. ____

____

____

APPLICATION: Activity 1

TRAVEL PLANS

Suppose Tuck lives in your back yard! Plan a daily travel route for him around your neighborhood. Label your yard, streets, points of interest, special bushes, and other things for Tuck's adventure in your neighborhood.

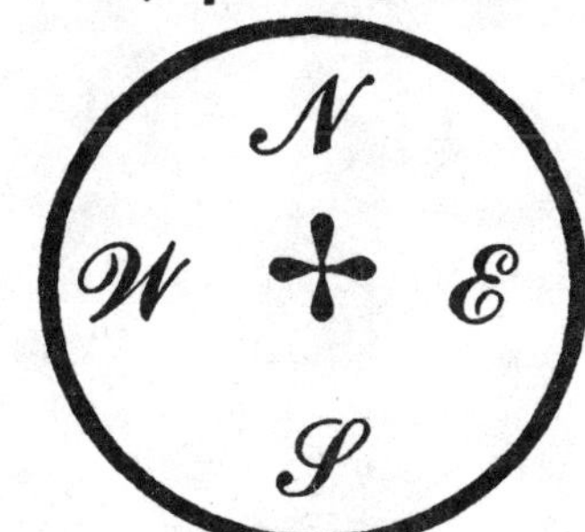

WHAT'S IT LIKE?

Helen wanted to know what it would be like to be blind. So, she closed her eyes very tightly and walked around her bedroom — bumping into the furniture and then tripping over Tuck!

Directions:

1. Try being "blind" for a day! Select a partner to help you in case you get into trouble, and to help you with your homework, etc.
2. Trade roles with your partner the next day.
3. Once each of you has had a day of being "blind," get together to find out what the other remembers most about the experience — and how he/she feels about it.

What I remember most about being "blind" for a day:

____

____

____

____

____

How I feel about being "blind" for a day:

____

____

____

____

____

BEST BUDDIES

Helen and Steffie have a lot in common. They both have braces and wear glasses. Both have freckles. Both consider themselves unattractive.

Do you know someone in your class who you think has a lot in common with you? ____________

Who? ____________________

Complete the following information.

1. Circle one:
   I am the only child in my house.
   I am the middle child in my house.
   I am the oldest child in my house.
   I am the youngest child in my house.
2. The flavor of ice cream that I like the best is __________.
3. My favorite sport is __________.
4. The color I like the best is __________.
5. The subject in school that interests me the most is __________.
6. My favorite book is __________.
7. One thing I really like to do in my free time is __________ __________.
8. My favorite animal is __________.
9. I like to watch __________ on television.
10. The song I like best is __________.
11. My favorite food to eat is __________.
12. A place I like to go is __________.

Now, compare your sheet with others in the class. Who do you have the most in common with?

____

ANALYSIS: Activity 2

MOMENTS

Answer and explain the following:

1. What part of the book is the *happiest*?

2. What part of the book is the *saddest*?

3. What part of the book is the *most frightening*?

4. What part of the book is the *most believable*?

5. What part of the book is the *most unbelievable*?

6. What part of the book is *like your life*?

GROWING UP IN THE FIFTIES

Helen grew up in the fifties. For a kid back then, it meant rock and roll with Elvis Presley, television with Howdy Doody, and breakfast with Tony the Tiger.

Plan a fifties party for your class.

1. After doing research in your library and interviewing people who grew up in the fifties, fill in the following party ideas. Don't forget to add any great ideas that you come up with that are not on this form.
2. Share your ideas with the rest of the class.
3. Set a date to have your party. Choose a party committee to organize everything you'll need. It might be a good idea to get a couple of parents to help out.

Food: ____________________

____

____

____

Games: ____________________

____

____

____

Records: ____________________

____

____

____

Clothes: ____________________

____

____

____

Other: ____

____

SYNTHESIS: Activity 2

MY PERFECT PET

If you could have the perfect pet, what would it look like? What would the two of you do together?

Below, draw a picture of the perfect pet for you. Then, on a separate paper, write a story about an adventure you have together. Read your story to the class as you show your pet's picture.

EVALUATION: Activity 1

THE NEW ME!

Looking back, Helen remembers her getting Tuck as being the turning point in her young life. That is, when she got Tuck, the direction in which her life had been going changed.

What has been a turning point in your life? ______________________

____

Explain. ______________________________________

____

____

____

MYSELF

Helen did not feel good about the way she looked or the way she acted.

1. Do you feel good about yourself?

2. Circle the things you like about yourself:

clothes	eyes	scholastic ability
teeth	height	personality
hair	athletic ability	weight

3. If you could change one thing about yourself, what would you change and why? ______________________________
____
____

4. Do you have friends? ________ How do you feel about your answer? ______________________________
____
____

5. Do you feel loved? __________ Explain. __________
____
____

6. Are you happy? __________ Explain. __________
____
____
____
____

Help! I'm a Prisoner in the Library

While driving through a blizzard with the gas gauge on empty, Mary Rose keeps telling her father to stop for gas before they run out. But, does Last-Minute Harry listen? No.

As soon as he leaves with the gas can from their trunk, Jo-Beth, Mary Rose's younger sister, declares she has to go to the bathroom. Disregarding their father's order to stay in the car, they fight their way through the wind and snow until they come to a library, just before it is to close.

The library is the first floor of an old mansion, the residence of Miss Vilmor Finton, the librarian. After Jo-Beth uses the rest room, the girls decide to investigate an exhibit they had seen when they first came in. Immersed in their curiosity, they don't notice Miss Finton closing up. When Miss Finton shuts off the main lights, the girls try to get help. But before they can, all the power goes out, leaving them alone together in a strange place — in the dark! And this strange place has strange noises, including the ones which come from the floor above.

Their investigation of the noises leads them to the unconscious body of Miss Finton who has tripped and hit her head when the power went off. Regaining consciousness, Miss Finton and the girls brave the mysteries of the dark, searching for a way to signal for help. During this time, Miss Finton tells them about the old mansion and shares the secrets of its many treasures.

WHAT CHARACTERS!

Write the letter of each character description under the name of the correct character.

a. was a woman who believed in carrying out her duties

b. never took care of anything until the very last minute

c. made a big deal out of everything

d. was a practical-minded girl

KNOWLEDGE: Activity 2

PICTURES IN TIME

Color and cut out these pictures. Paste them on a separate piece of paper in story order.

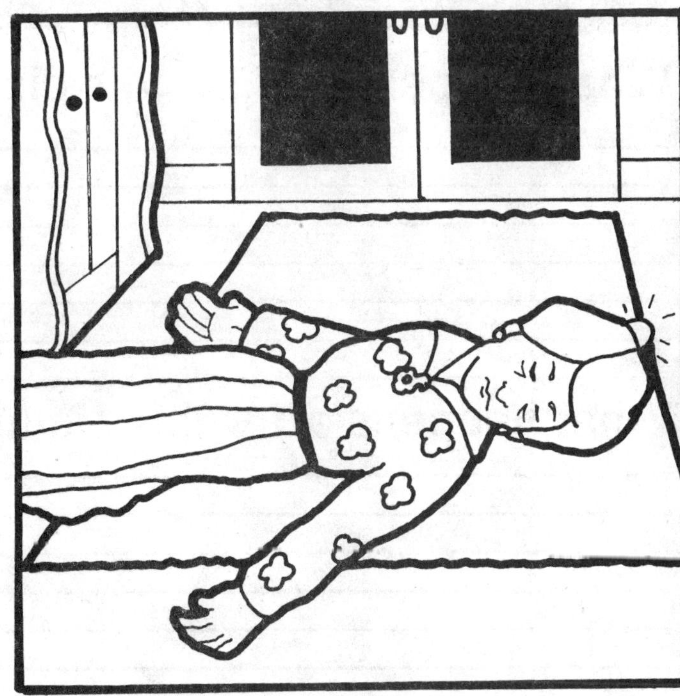

BEFORE AND AFTER

What happens **before** this picture in the story? ______

What happens **after** this picture in the story? ______

A PERFECTLY REASONABLE EXPLANATION

Jo-Beth imagines the worst each time she hears or sees something unusual in the library. Miss Finton advises Jo-Beth to control her imagination. She assures Jo-Beth that everything has a perfectly reasonable explanation.

What are the "perfectly reasonable explanations" for these things Jo-Beth imagines she hears or sees in the story.

1. bats: ______________________________

____

____

2. the ghostly movement of papers that makes Jo-Beth think the house is haunted: ______________

____

____

____

____

____

3. a banshee: ______________________________

____

____

____

____

____

APPLICATION: Activity 1

GET US OUT!

Mary Rose tried to call the police for help. The police sergeant thought she was playing a joke and hung up on her. What would **you** have said to the police officer to **make** him believe your call for help?

Can you think of any other ways to get out of the library? Remember, the librarian has the door key and the phone is dead.

PUPPET SHOW!

(See page 58 for directions.)

- Make paper bag puppets for Miss Finton, Mary Rose, and Jo-Beth.
- In groups of three, plan a conversation that the three of them could have.
- Perform your Puppet Show for the class.

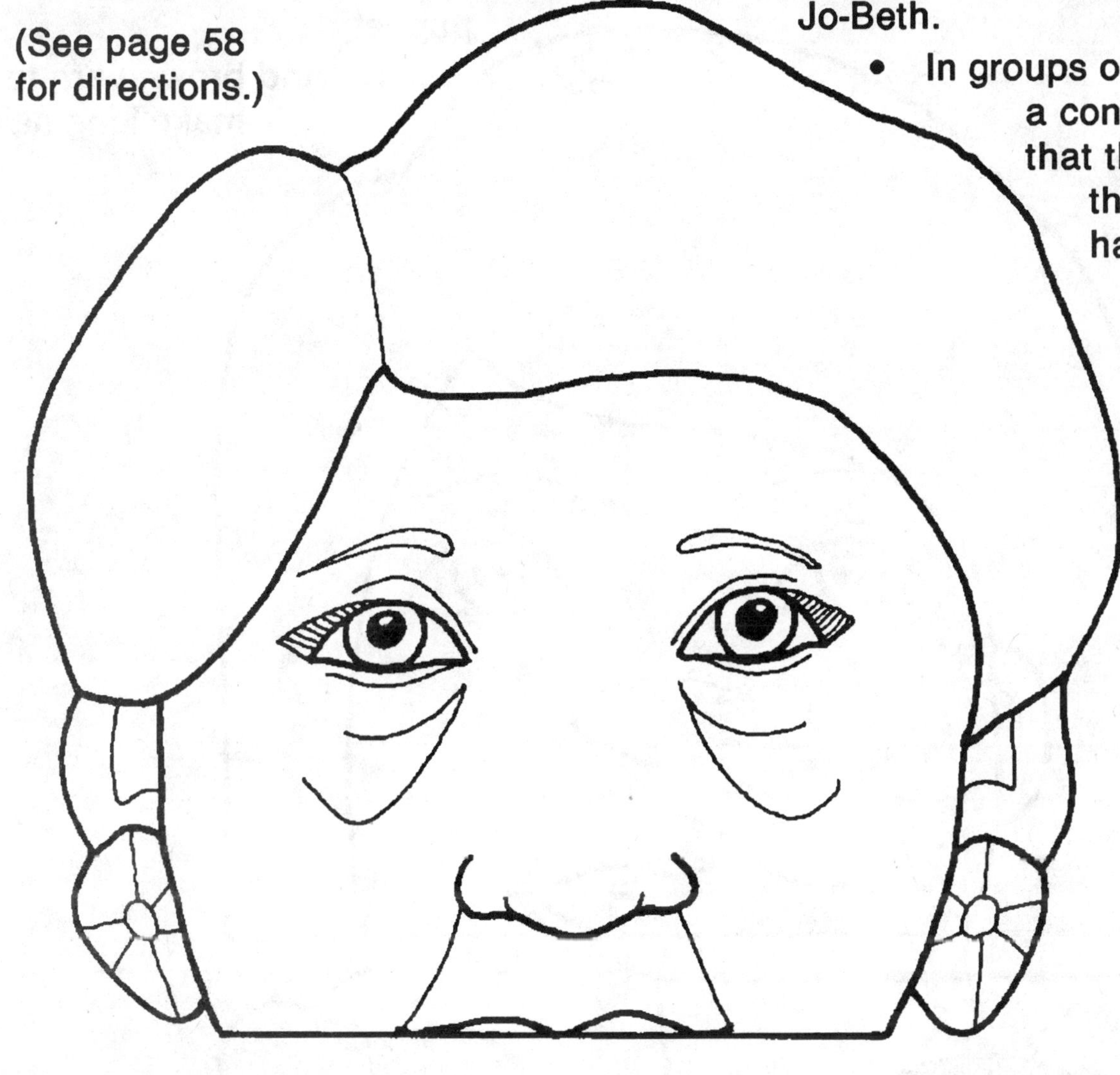

Miss Finton

 GROUP PROJECT

PUPPET SHOW!

1. Color and cut out.
2. Glue to paper bag to make puppet.
3. Add brown yarn to make long hair.

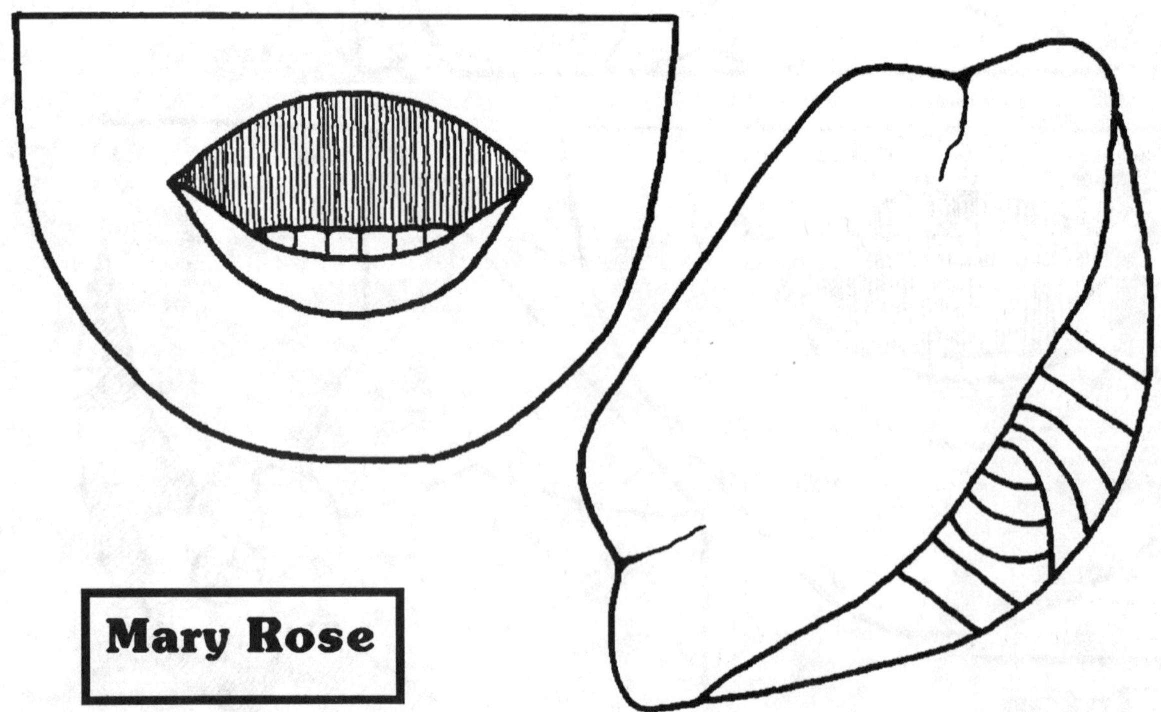

Mary Rose

APPLICATION: Activity 2 (Page 3 of 3)

GROUP PROJECT

PUPPET SHOW!

1. Color and cut out.
2. Glue to paper bag to make puppet.
3. Add brown yarn to make long hair.

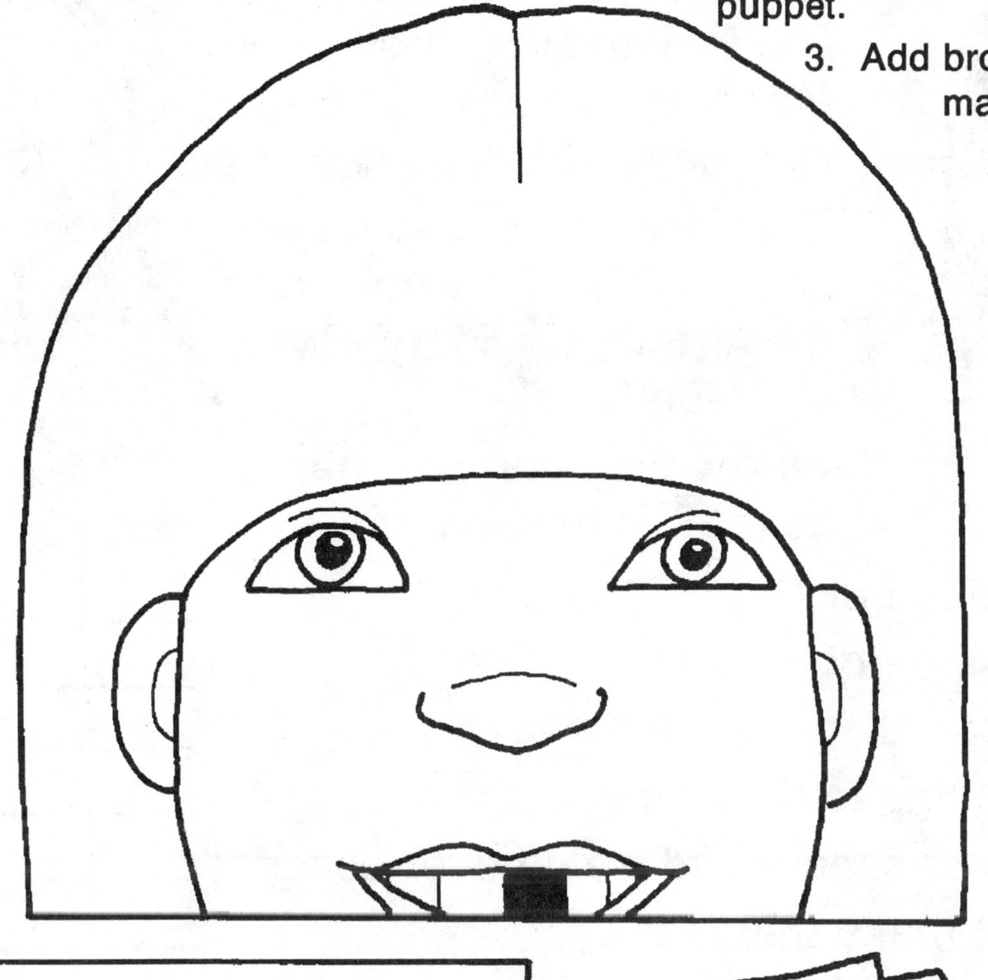

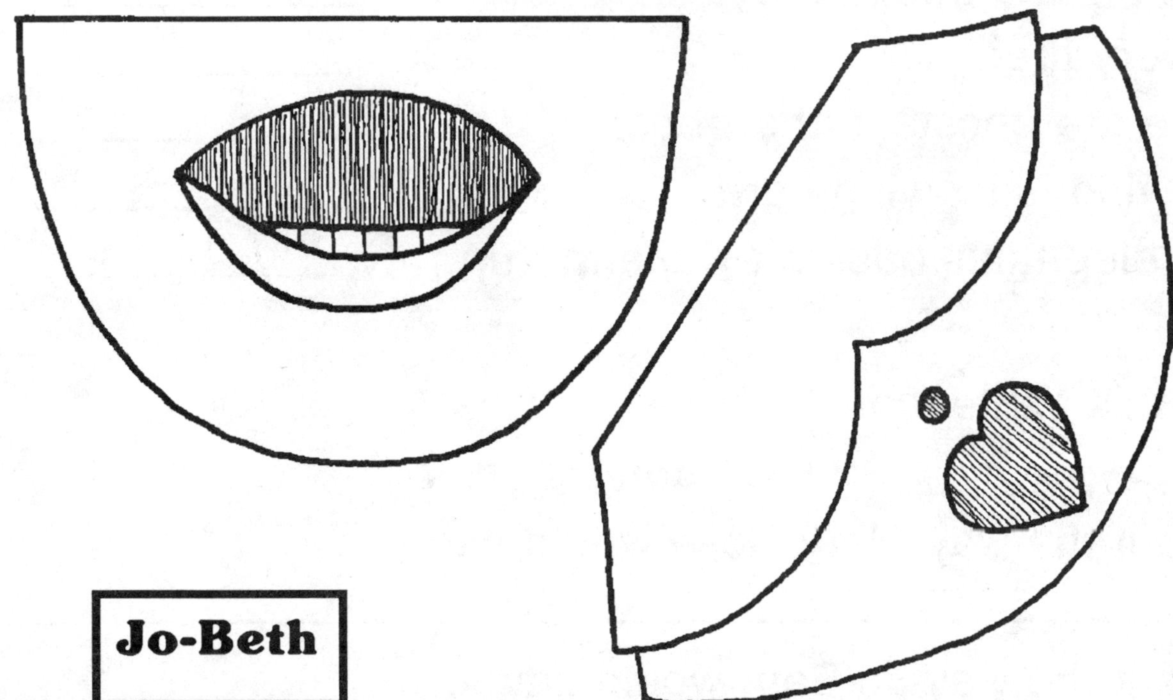

Jo-Beth

ANALYSIS: Activity 1

MARY ROSE OR JO-BETH?

After reading the story, do you feel that you know how Mary Rose and Jo-Beth see the world?

Read the sentences below and decide who would say these things: Mary Rose or Jo-Beth.

Write the correct name next to each sentence.

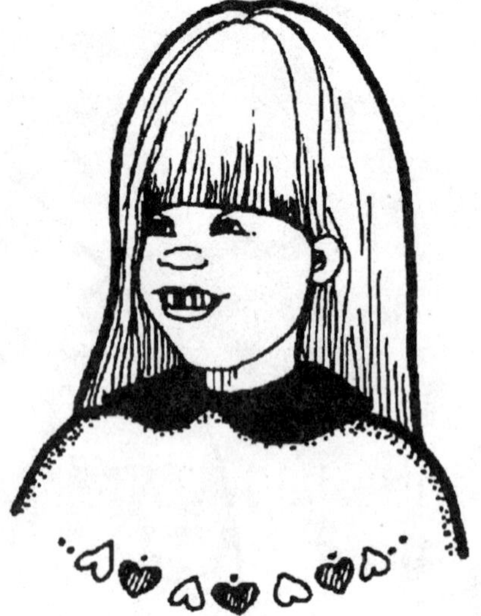

1. We will surely freeze to death! ________________
2. We will be quite cold. ________________
3. I'm scared. ________________
4. I am going to die of fright! ________________
5. We're prisoners and we'll never escape! ________________
6. I don't make things up. ________________
7. I'm very tired. ________________
8. There are ghosts in the trees. ________________
9. The wind is blowing hard. ________________
10. Wild elephants couldn't wake me up. ________________

Look at this sentence.

I am hungry.

✓ Write it the way Mary Rose would say it.

____

✓ Write it the way Jo-Beth would say it.

____

ANALYSIS: Activity 2

YES OR NO?

Help! I'm a Prisoner in the Library! is based on two experiences the author, Eth Clifford, had in her own life: being trapped by a terrible blizzard in Indianapolis and visiting the Rauh Memorial Library as a child.

Could these things from the story happen to you? Write "yes" or "no" next to each one.

1. Your mother is going to have a baby. ________
2. Your father is driving and runs out of gas. ________
3. You have to go to the bathroom and just can't wait. ________
4. You get very interested in a library display. ________
5. You hear a mynah bird talk. ________
6. You hear noises that frighten you. ________
7. You explore something new, even though it might be dangerous. ________
8. You help an injured person because you know some first aid. ________
9. You eat food from someone's refrigerator without asking. ________
10. You rescue a cat from a place it is trapped. ________
11. You like looking at storybook characters. ________
12. You have an idea that could make someone's future very happy. ________

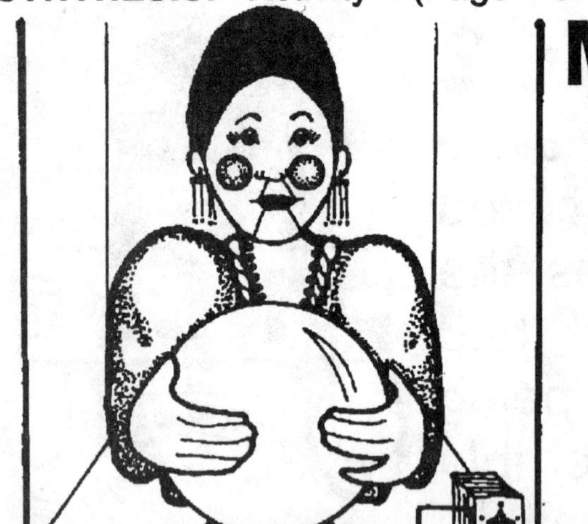

MADAME MORGANA!

Make a fortune-teller machine like the one in the story, using a box large enough to house a classmate. Select one person at a time from your class to dress up like Madame Morgana and wear the "Madame Morgana" mask.

Each class member writes a fortune to give to the class fortune teller. The class fortune teller shuffles the fortunes and distibutes them to class members — for a penny or not!

Example of fortune:

"Strange things will happen to you in a place of mystery. You will fear for your life, but you will be saved. Tell no one of your adventures. They will not believe you."

Your fortune for Madame Morgana's machine:

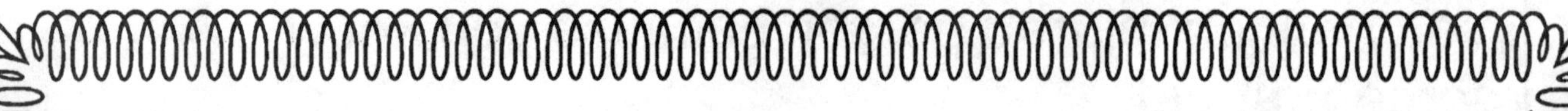

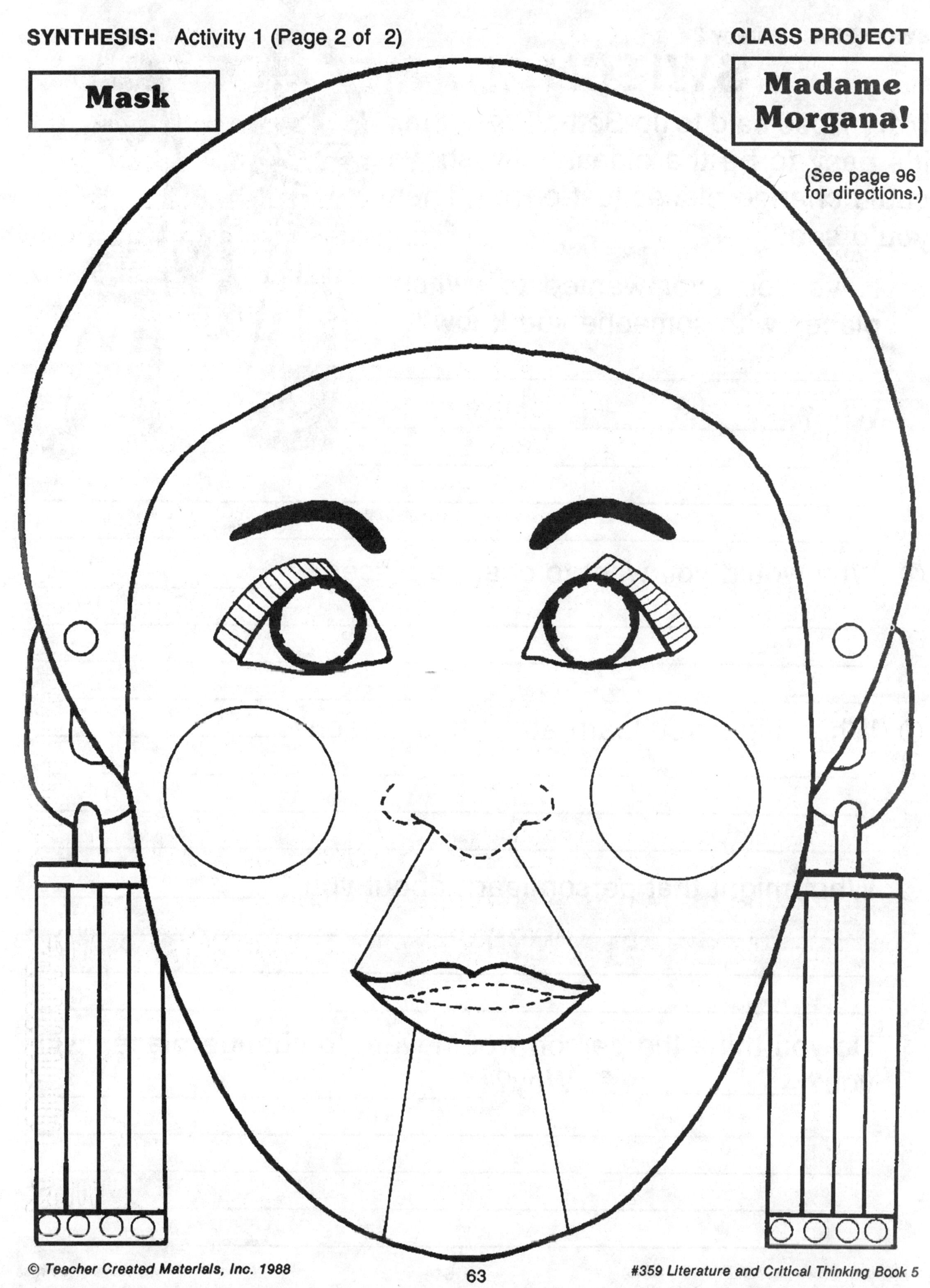

(See page 96 for directions.)

SYNTHESIS: Activity 2

SWITCH

Mary Rose said to Jo-Beth, "You think it's easy to be the oldest? I wish we could change places just once. Then you'd see."

① Have you ever wanted to switch places with someone you know?

____

Who? ______________________________

____

____

____

② Why would you want to change places? ______________

____

____

____

③ What might you learn about this person? ______________

____

____

____

④ What might that person learn about you? ______________

____

____

____

⑤ Do you think the person would want to change places with you? ____________ Why? ______________

____

____

____

____

EVALUATION: Activity 1

WERE THEY RIGHT?

Two decisions were made by people in the story that greatly affected the girls' stay in the library. You decide if these people made the right decisions.

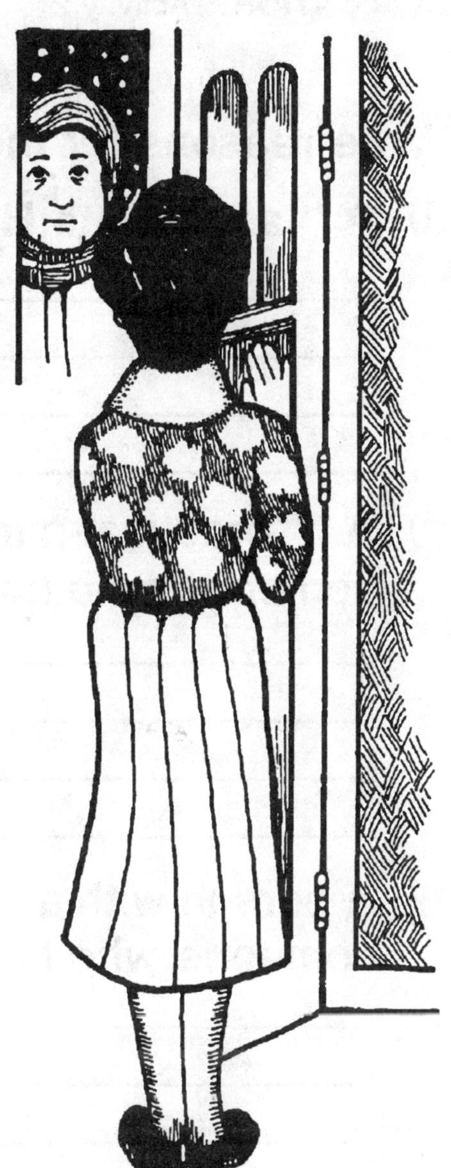

① Miss Finton would not let Mr. Onetree into the library to look for his girls.

Was she right? ____________________

Why? ____________________

____

____

____

____

____

____

____

____

② The police officer who receives Mary Rose's call for help hangs up on her.

Was he right? ____________________

Why? ____________________

____

____

____

____

____

____

READ THIS BOOK!

Write reasons for the following people to read this book.

① A "last-minute Harry" type of person: ____________________

② A "practical-minded" person who doesn't appreciate someone who has a "vivid imagination": ____________________

③ A person with a "vivid imagination" who doesn't appreciate someone who is "practical-minded": ____________________

④ A person who doesn't believe in taking "unnecessary chances": ____________________

⑤ A person too quick to suspect prank phone calls: ____________________

Call It Courage

by Armstrong Sperry

The early Polynesians worshiped courage, and a person who was afraid had no place with them.

Such is the case with Mafatu, a boy who fears the sea. Mafatu is the laughing stock of the girls and boys in his fishing village, and a source of shame for his father. So, he decides to conquer his fear of the sea — to find those things outside and inside himself that will be a testament to his courage.

When he arrives on a far-away island, he builds a shelter, fashions weapons, provides food for himself and his dog Uri, and makes a canoe. But, in the process, he discovers that the island is a place of human sacrifice, worshiped by the feared eaters-of-men.

What Mafatu does on this island, and on his return journey home, helps him to conquer his fear of the sea, and to take his rightful place among his people as one with ***courage***!

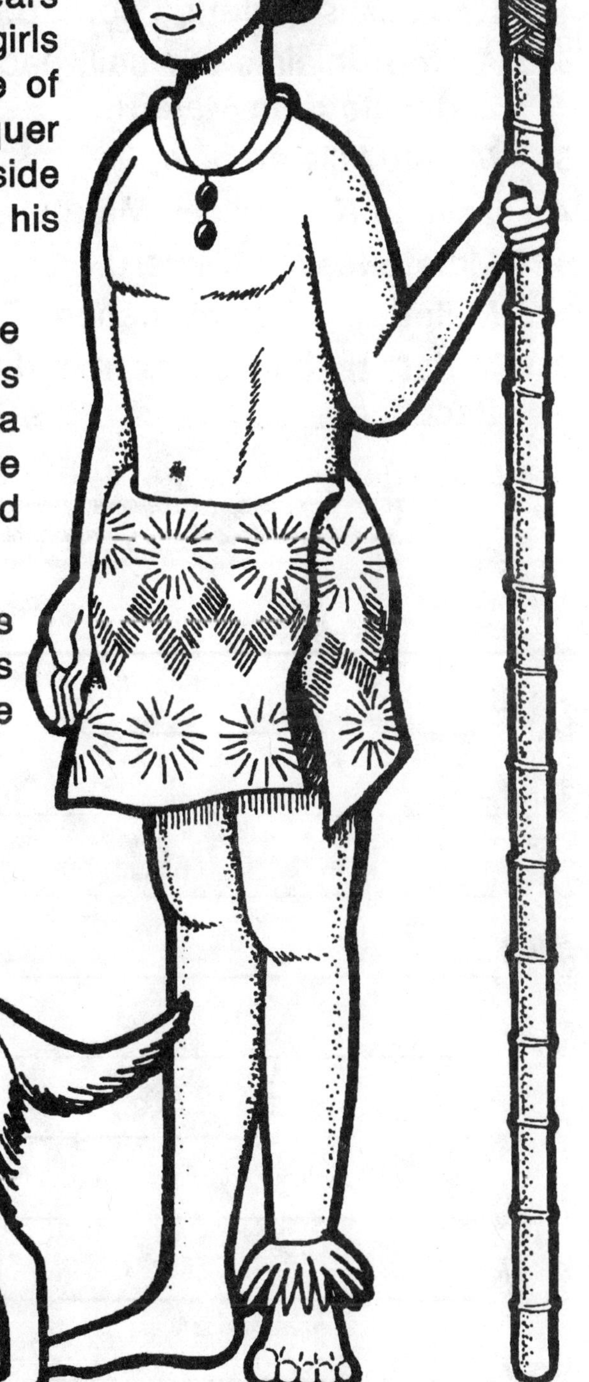

KNOWLEDGE: Activity 1

EVENTS IN ORDER

Write these events from the story in the order they happen.

1. The eaters-of-men chase Mafatu.
2. Mafatu's mother dies.
3. Mafatu kills the wild pig.
4. Kana calls Mafatu a coward.
5. A storm claims the sail, paddle, food, and knife from Mafatu.
6. Mafatu kills an octopus.
7. Tavana Nui praises Mafatu.
8. Mafatu leaves Hikueru.
9. Mafatu finishes his canoe.
10. Mafatu takes a spear from the Place of Sacrifice.

① #______ ________________________________

② #______ ________________________________

③ #______ ________________________________

④ #______ ________________________________

⑤ #______ ________________________________

⑥ #______ ________________________________

⑦ #______ ________________________________

⑧ #______ ________________________________

⑨ #______ ________________________________

⑩ #______ ________________________________

KNOWLEDGE: Activity 2

CHARACTER QUOTES

Match these quotes with the characters who said them.

Moana	Tavana Nui
Kana	Mafatu

1. "Mafatu, Stout Heart. A brave name for a brave boy!"

   ____

2. "I have tried to be friendly with him. But he is good only for making spears. Mafatu is a coward."

   ____

3. "Do you hear me, Moana? I am not afraid of you! Destroy me — but I laugh at you. Do you hear? I **laugh**."

   ____

4. "Someday, someday, Mafatu, I will claim you."

   ____

5. "Maui! Do not desert me," he prayed, "This last time — lend me your help."

   ____

6. "Ho! That is woman's work. Mafatu is afraid of the sea. He will never be a warrior."

   ____

COMPREHENSION: Activity 1

THE SEA

Explain how Mafatu feels about the sea in the beginning, middle, and end of the story.

BEGINNING

MIDDLE

END

COMPREHENSION: Activity 2

WHAT DO THESE MEAN?

What do these mean to Mafatu in the story?

1. Uri: ______

2. Kivi: ______

3. Moana: ______

4. The boar-tusk necklace: ______

5. Whale bones: ______

6. Thump-thump THUMP of a drumbeat: ______

7. Mafatu's canoe: ______

APPLICATION: Activity 1

MEAL FOR MAFATU

When Mafatu is on the island, we learn about the types of food available to him and what he really likes.

Plan a complete meal for Mafatu. Use the food you know or think he will like.

Restaurant Mafatu

appetizers:

____

____

____

main course:

____

____

____

____

____

____

____

dessert:

____

____

____

____

beverage:

____

____

____

APPLICATION: Activity 2

JUST SUPPOSE . . .

Just suppose Mafatu does not hear Kana call him a coward. Just suppose Mafatu never leaves Hikueru to prove his courage.

What do you think Mafatu's life will be like on Hikueru? Write a diary account of a typical day in his life.

ANALYSIS

1 What part of the story do you think is the most frightening? ______

2 In what part of the story do you think Mafatu shows the most courage? ______

3 What part of the story do you think is the most believable? ______

4 What part of the story do you think is the most unbelievable? ______

5 In what part of the story does Mafatu do something that you would do also? ______

ANALYSIS: Activity 2

WHAT IS COURAGE?

> Courage is very important to the people of Hikueru, especially Mafatu. Braving the sea alone, touching the marae (sacred place) to possess a spear, killing a wild boar singlehandedly — these are signs of courage to Mafatu and his people.

What is courage to you? Analyze the actions below. Underline the ones that take courage to do.

1. eating something you have never tried before
2. standing up for a friend when others are teasing him
3. rescuing a drowning person
4. reading a book from cover to cover
5. apologizing to a teacher for creating a disturbance in class
6. saving a kitten from the jaws of a dog
7. sleeping with the light off when you have been afraid of the dark
8. telling your neighbor that you broke his window with a baseball
9. doing something you want to do, even though your friends think what you want to do is unpopular or silly
10. studying for a test instead of watching your favorite TV show

Now write three things that **you** think take courage to do.

1. ____________________

2. ____________________

3. ____________________

MAFATU, STOUT HEART!

With your class, write a song to praise the courage of Mafatu. You may put your words to a melody you already know or create music of your own. Learn the song as a class and sing it for an assembly or parents' meeting!

Write your song here.

EATERS-OF-MEN

From Mafatu's observations and thoughts, we know what the eaters-of-men do. But we do not know what they think or say.

With a partner, write a conversation that the eaters-of-men may have had that night they discovered Mafatu on their island of sacrifice.

EVALUATION: Activity 1

YOU ARE THE JUDGE!

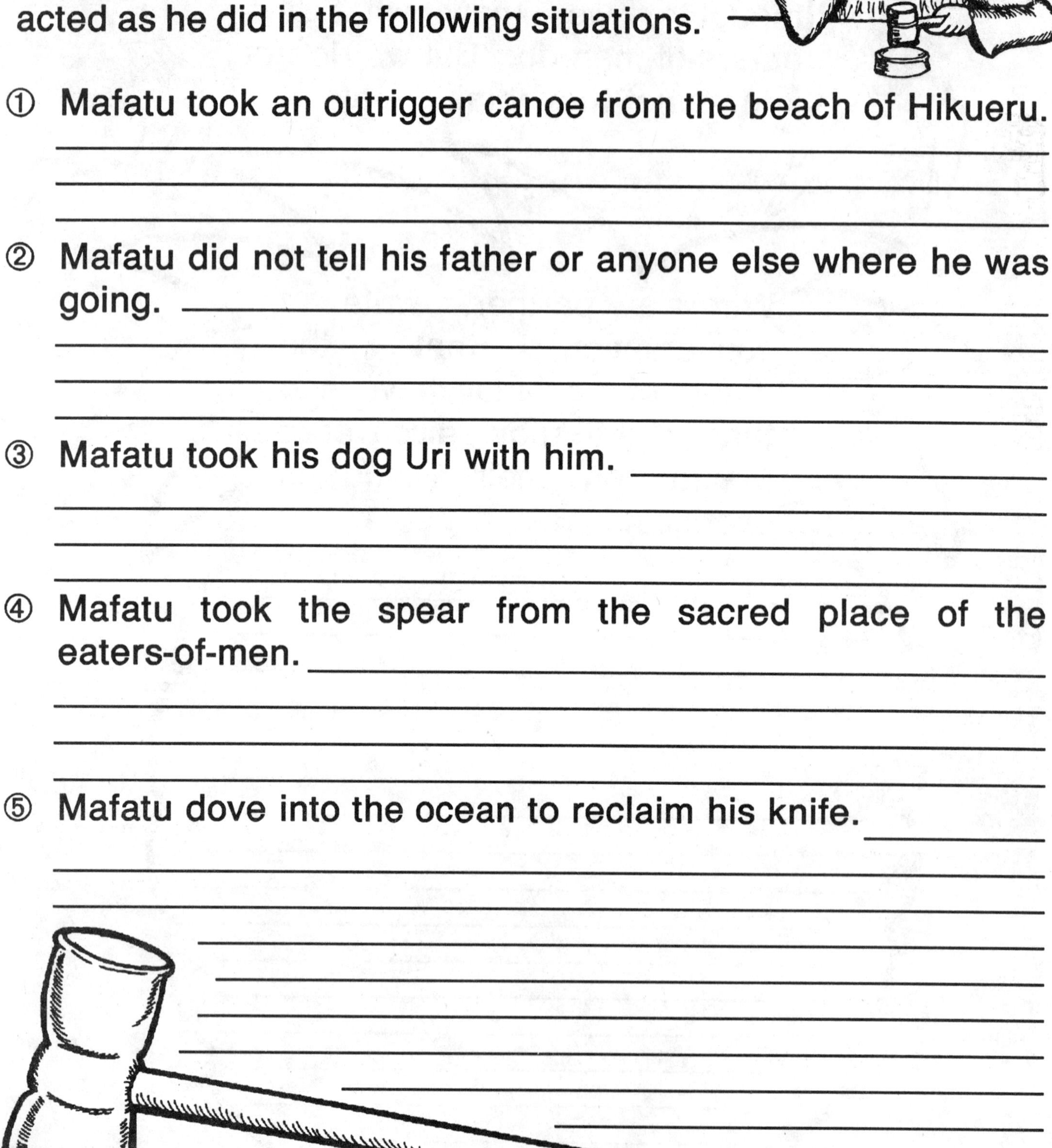

Judge whether or not Mafatu should have acted as he did in the following situations.

① Mafatu took an outrigger canoe from the beach of Hikueru.

② Mafatu did not tell his father or anyone else where he was going.

③ Mafatu took his dog Uri with him.

④ Mafatu took the spear from the sacred place of the eaters-of-men.

⑤ Mafatu dove into the ocean to reclaim his knife.

EVALUATION: Activity 2

FEAR

1 Do you understand why Mafatu had a fear of the sea? __________Explain your answer. ____________________

2 Do you think Mafatu's fear is justified? __________
Explain your answer. ____________________

3 Is there something that frightens you? __________
Explain your answer. ____________________

4 Have you been teased because of a fear you have had? __________If so, explain how the teasing made you feel.

5 Have you tried to overcome a fear you have had? _____
Explain your answer. ____________________

Be a Perfect Person in Just Three Days

by Stephen Manes

Milo Crinkley only wanted one thing in life — to be a perfect person. Then, one day while in the library looking for a monster story to read, a book fell off the shelf and hit him on the head. He read the title — *Be A Perfect Person In Just Three Days*.

From that moment on, Milo found it impossible to put the book down, even though the author, Dr. K. Pinkerton Silverfish, had his reader do some pretty strange things. In his quest for perfection, Milo agreed to do things like wear a necklace made of broccoli, go without eating for 24 hours, and finally, do absolutely nothing for another 24 hours (except for going to the bathroom and sipping weak tea slowly). These, of course, were things that inspired ridicule and questioning from nearly everyone — from his sister Elissa to his friends at school.

In the end, Milo came to the conclusion that being a perfect person was not all that he thought it would be. Being perfect, he decided, was boring and no fun. Dr. Silverfish could have told him that on page 1, but Milo just had to find it out for himself!

KNOWLEDGE: Activity 1

WHO SAID THIS?

Match these quotes with the characters who said them.

❶ "Well, maybe I'm not as stupid as I look. After all, I guessed what you were thinking, didn't I?"

Said by: ______________________________

❷ "I don't know if I could stand living with a perfect person."

Said by: ______________________________

❸ "I bet you'd love me if I turned perfect."

Said by: ______________________________

❹ "If you ask me, I've got a broccoli-brain for a brother."

Said by: ______________________________

KNOWLEDGE: Activity 2

ORDER, PLEASE!

Here are pictures of six things that happen in the story. Number them 1 through 6 in the order that they happen.

#___

#___

#___

#___

#___

#___

COMPREHENSION: Activity 1

BEFORE AND AFTER

At the **beginning** of the story, does Milo want to be a perfect person? ____________

Why? ____

____

____

____

____

____

____

At the **end** of the story, does Milo want to be a perfect person? ____________

Why? ____

____

____

____

____

____

____

COMPREHENSION: Activity 2

IN YOUR WORDS . . .

Explain these ideas from the story in your own words.

① "It is a well-known fact that there is nothing in the entire world more humiliating than wearing a stalk of broccoli around your neck. So just think, you have nothing more to fear for the rest of your life." *(Chapter 4)* ____________________

____

____

____

② "But you have proven that even if you think something's nearly impossible, like learning Finnish or becoming a classical kazoo player or building a model of the Eiffel Tower out of chewing gum, you'll be able to stick to it and get it done if you really want to." *(Chapter 5)* ____________________

____

____

____

③ "If you never dropped a ball or struck out, baseball would be as boring as sipping weak tea." *(Chapter 6)*

____

____

____

____

____

APPLICATION: Activity 1 (Page 1 of 2)

TIME TO EAT!

Draw a meal that a perfect person would love to eat.

Describe how he or she would eat it.

____

____

____

____

____

TIME TO EAT!

Draw a meal that a person who is not perfect would love to eat.

Describe how he or she would eat it. ______________

____

____

____

____

APPLICATION: Activity 2

PROBLEMS

Milo wants to be perfect. He thinks that being perfect will solve his problems.

Here are five problems Milo seems to have. Give examples of people you know who have the same problems as Milo.

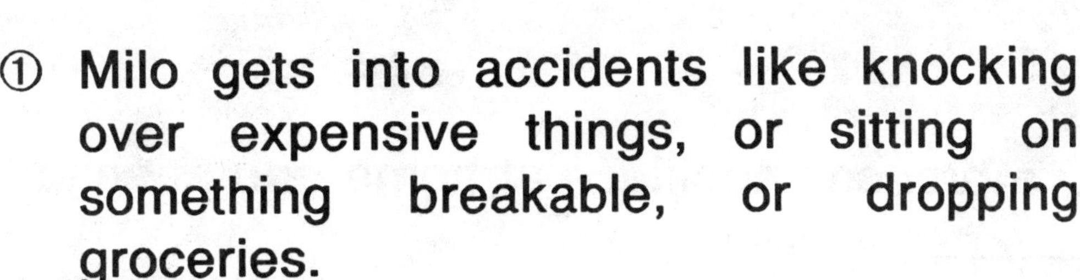

① Milo gets into accidents like knocking over expensive things, or sitting on something breakable, or dropping groceries.

People: ______________________________

____

② Milo has a sister who fights with him.

People: ______________________________

____

③ Milo backs away from a bully who teases him.

People: ______________________________

____

④ Milo is a messy eater.

People: ______________________________

____

⑤ Milo is not a very good ball player, but he still likes to play.

People: ______________________________

____

ANALYSIS: Activity 1

ME, TOO!

You want to be perfect, just like Milo. You find the same book and read it.

Would you be able to do the things that Milo did? Answer each question honestly.

1. Could you wear a broccoli necklace at home and at school for one day? ____________

   Explain: ____
   ____
   ____
   ____

2. Could you not eat or drink anything except water for 24 hours straight? ____________

   Explain: ____
   ____
   ____
   ____

3. Could you do nothing for 24 hours straight, except go to the bathroom, sip weak tea slowly, and breathe? ____________

   Explain: ____
   ____
   ____
   ____

PERFECT OR NOT?

What do perfect people do? What do people who are not perfect do?

Read this list of things people do. Write **PERFECT** if perfect people do it. Write **NOT PERFECT** if people who are not perfect do it.

1. Never use an eraser: ____________________
2. Drop bags of groceries: ____________________
3. Fight with a brother or sister: ____________________
4. Get perfect scores on all tests: ____________________
5. Eat too fast: ____________________
6. Stub toes: ____________________
7. Cut food into bite-sized pieces: ____________________
8. Lock keys in the car: ____________________
9. Say "Thank you" without being told to: ____________________
10. Dribble ketchup down your chin: ____________________
11. Strike out at baseball: ____________________
12. Sit completely still: ____________________

Class Story

You are about to read a book called ***Be A Perfect Person In Just Three Days***! But, before you read it, you and your classmates are going to make up a story from just the title.

Write your story idea here.

Share your idea with the class.

Class Story

After you have heard the ideas from all your classmates, write your favorite idea here. ______________________________

____

____

____

____

____

Who had this idea? ______________________________

The class will select one idea and begin to tell a story. Each class member may add ideas to the main story idea.

Write the main story idea here. ______________________

____

____

____

____

____

Who had this idea? ______________________

What are some ideas the class added to the main idea? ______________________

____

____

Did you make a good story? ____________

THE PLAN

How can a person become perfect? You create the plan! Work in groups of 2 or 3 to make a plan for perfection!

How To Become Perfect

by ______________________
____
____

1. Length of time it takes: ______________________
____
2. Special things needed to make the plan work: ______________________
____
____
3. Steps to perfection: ______________________
____
____
____
____
____
4. Will this plan work for everyone? ______________________
____
5. Is the perfection permanent? ______________________
Explain. ______________________
____
____

PERFECT YOU!

Would **you** like to be perfect?

➥ Give 2 reasons why you would like to be perfect.

❶ ____

____

❷ ____

____

➥ Give 2 reasons why you would not like to be perfect.

❶ ____

____

❷ ____

____

➥ How could being perfect help your relationships with family and friends? Give 2 ways.

❶ ____

❷ ____

➥ How could being perfect hurt your relationships with family and friends? Give 2 ways.

❶ ____

❷ ____

➥ Do you want to be perfect?__________Why?________________

____

EVALUATION: Activity 2

DR. K. PINKERTON SILVERFISH

1. Why do you think Dr. Silverfish has Milo do the things he does to become perfect?

   a. Wear a broccoli necklace: ____________

   b. Eat no food for 24 hours: ____________

   c. Do nothing for 24 hours: ____________

2. Do you think Dr. Silverfish knew Milo would fail? ____________

   Explain: ____________

3. Is Dr. Silverfish perfect? ____________

   How do you know? ____________

4. Is anyone perfect? ____________

   Explain your answer. ____________

ANSWER KEY

HOW TO EAT FRIED WORMS

K-1 1) Billy 2) Alan 3) Joe 4) Tom
K-2 numbers circled: 2, 3, 4, 5, 7, 10
numbers not circled: 1, 6, 8, 9
C-1 BEFORE: Alan and Joe decide to stuff Billy with food at a baseball game and tire him out with this late trip to the extent that he will be so full and sleepy that he will miss eating his daily worm.
AFTER: Billy awakens, realizes the trick, and, with the help of Tom and Pete, finds and eats a worm on time, alerting Alan, Joe, and the whole neighborhood to his feat.
C-2
1. Billy doesn't think it fair that the worm chosen is a huge nightcrawler. He protests as best he can, but his first feast will be the "dictionary-defined" worm.
2. Alan and Joe, who try to trick a sleepy and full Billy into forgetting his worm for the day, are alerted by a blaring siren that Billy is on to them. The siren awakens all the neighbors, and Billy yells that Alan and Joe are to blame, thus prompting a parental punishment for the tricksters as well as a neighborhood apology.
3. Billy has developed a real liking for worms and can't stop eating them, even after the bet has been won!

S-2 Brainstorm ideas such as these with the class:
Once he starts to eat a worm, how long does Billy have to finish eating it?
What are the rules of conduct for people who wish to observe Billy as he eats a worm?
Where must Billy eat the worm?
What is the definition of "worm"?
What size worm must Billy eat (minimum and maximum size)?
What size bites must Billy take when he eats a worm?
What is Billy allowed to put on the worm, and in what quantity?
When must Alan pay Billy if Billy wins the bet?
Etc.

THE WHIPPING BOY

K-1 Down 1) Cutwater 2) Jemmy 4) Prince Horace 5) King 6) Nips 9) Brat
Across 3) Master Peckwit 7) Billy 8) Betsy 10) Johnny Tosher 11) Petunia 12) Smudge
K-2
1) making mischief: Prince Brat
2) running away: Prince Brat and Jemmy
3) ransom note: Billy and Jemmy
4) whipping and rescue: Billy, Prince Brat (Horace), and Petunia
5) thieves and rats: Billy and Cutwater
6) friends: King, Prince Horace, and Jemmy

C-1 1) b 2) a 3) a 4) c 5) a 6) c 7) b 8) c
C-2
1) Jemmy was very angry with the Prince for giving away his hiding place. Their escape would have been much easier had the Prince not revealed Jemmy's spot. It also showed Jemmy that he could not trust the Prince, etc.
2) The Prince took a whipping for Jemmy and did not cry out in pain. Jemmy had wanted to see the Prince punished, but he was sad to see it happening, not glad, etc.
3) The King would like to go on an adventure with the boys. Perhaps his life needed some "thrills," etc.

App-1 Check for appropriateness.
App-2 Check for appropriateness.
An-1 Alike: boys, proud, brave, kind (although the Prince took a while to show it), adventurous, etc.
Different: poor/rich, interested in learning/not interested in learning, street-wise/foolish, practical/trickster, etc.
Answers will vary.
An-2 Prince Horace and Jemmy's friendship grew because of: mutual respect, need, devotion, experiences shared, etc.

THE TROUBLE WITH TUCK

K-1 1) 4 2) 5 3) 1 4) 2 5) 3
K-2 1) f 2) j 3) d 4) a 5) h 6) g 7) c 8) k 9) e 10) l 11) i 12) b
C-1 Mr. Ogden gives Helen the puppy to help her build her self-confidence.
C-2 Tuck: 1) saves Helen from the rapist
2) saves Helen from drowning

ANSWER KEY (Continued)

THE TROUBLE WITH TUCK

3) builds her self-confidence
4) is her steadfast friend, etc.

Helen: 1) takes good care of Tuck's dog needs
2) goes "out on a limb" to find him a seeing eye dog
3) defends him against all misfortune
4) trains him even though he resists quite obstinately, etc.

HELP! I'M A PRISONER IN THE LIBRARY!

K-1 Jo-Beth - c Vilmor Finton - a
Mr. Onetree - b Mary Rose - d

K-2 1) gas gauge 2) body 3) fireworks 4) sign in dream

C-1 Before: Last-Minute Harry neglects to gas up and runs out of gas in a snowstorm, etc.
After: Jo-Beth has to go to the bathroom and the girls go inside the Finton Memorial Library, etc.

C-2 1. The "bats" turn out to be Miss Finton's pet mynah bird.
2. "Paper ghosts" are caused by the draft of air from the open basement door.
3. The "banshee" is a wailing cat, caught in a basement window.

An-1 1) Jo-Beth 2) Mary Rose 3) Mary Rose 4) Jo-Beth 5) Jo-Beth 6) Mary Rose 7) Mary Rose 8) Jo-Beth 9) Mary Rose 10) Jo-Beth

An-2 The answers will be based on the child's view of reality. They all could be "yes."

S-1 1) Color mask 2) Cut out eye and mouth holes 3) Cut out mask. Cut nose along dotted lines. 4) Stick several layers of tape on and behind holes for attaching mask. Then punch out holes and tie yarn through holes.

CALL IT COURAGE

K-1 1) 2 2) 4 3) 8 4) 5 5) 10 6) 3 7) 9 8) 6 9) 1 10) 7

K-2 1) Tavana Nui 2) Kana 3) Mafatu 4) Moana 5) Mafatu 6) Kana

C-1 Beginning: Mafatu fears the sea and his fear of it stops him from joining other boys his age on their way to becoming fishermen, etc.
Middle: Mafatu still fears the sea, but has begun to realize that it does not have to be his enemy, etc.
End: Mafatu has conquered his fear of the sea and has become "one" with it, etc.

C-2 1. Uri is Mafatu's faithful yellow dog, who follows him everywhere. Mafatu loves Uri deeply, etc.
2. Kivi is an albatross, befriended by Mafatu when the limping bird is heckled away from his flock. Mafatu is kind and loving to Kivi, etc.
3. Moana, the Sea God, is responsible — or so Mafatu thinks — for his mother's death, his ostracism from his people, his bad fortune on the sea, etc. Mafatu hates Moana, until the end when he laughs at the god and his fear, etc.
4. The boar-tusk necklace is symbolic of Mafatu's bravery, for he has to kill a wild board singlehandedly to get it. Mafatu knows all will respect his courage when they see the necklace, etc.
5. Whale bones mean many weapons for Mafatu. He feels he is rich when he discovers them, etc.
6. The thumping of the drumbeat means that the eaters-of-men have landed on the island where Mafatu is, and he must leave — immediately! etc.
7. Mafatu's canoe is his pride. He has worked long and hard to make it right, and it is, etc.

A-2 Each item on the list can be supported as a courageous activity.

BE A PERFECT PERSON IN JUST THREE DAYS

K-1 1) Dr. Silverfish 2) Mr. Crinkley 3) Milo 4) Elissa

K-2 1) book 2) broccoli 3) not eating 4) "Do Not Disturb" 5) weak tea 6) striking out

C-1 Beginning: yes, he thinks it would be great – no hassles at home; perfect, brilliant work at school, etc.
End: no, he thinks it would be boring – no drips, trips, or excitement, etc.

C-2 1) If Milo has the courage to face his world wearing a stalk of broccoli, he has the courage to face anything, etc.
2) If Milo can have the will power to go without eating for 24 hours, he has the will power to do what he wants to do, etc.
3) If people are perfect, with no risks or mistakes ever, they lead a very boring life, etc.

An-2 Perfect: 1, 4, 7, 9, 12
Not Perfect: 2, 3, 5, 6, 8, 10, 11

